POMPEII
ON MY MIND

Pompeii on My Mind

NILDA CEPERO

House of the Tragic Poet

Other books by Nilda Cepero:

Poetry
Sugar Cane Blues
Lil' Havana Blues
A Blues Cantata
Bohemian Canticles
Hemingway, The Last Daiquiri
Short Stories
Más Allá del Azul
Memoirs
Recuerdos de Sevilla y otros caminos
A mi gusto: La cocina de las "muchachitas"
    (bilingual)
Paris Always Paris

Front and back cover: *Fresco from Casa dei Casti Amanti*
(House of the Chaste Lovers)

ISBN 978-1-890953-16-4

Grief has limits, whereas apprehension has none. For we grieve only for what we know has happened, but we fear all that possibly may happen.

— Pliny the Elder
[Died during the eruption while rescuing a friend]

To E Jerry with love, who didn't fail the test and has made all my exciting trips possible; to Yasmin, who has the courage to enjoy traveling the world; and to Juanita, a perfect traveling companion, who taught me that life is what we make it to be.

INTRODUCTION

Years ago, moved by the scene unfolding in front of my eyes, I walked the dusty roads of Pompeii. Immersed in this heart-stirring find, I metamorphosed into part of the story. I had gone through piles of photographs, but being there was a consciousness-altering experience like no other. In other words, you have to be there to grasp the importance of these ancient ruins.

Before visiting the area, I learned that Pompeii had been a city located near Naples (Napoli) in the Campania region, the regional capital and the third-largest city of Italy. But in 79 AD, Pompeii was buried in the eruption of Mount Vesuvius together with nearby Herculaneum and other smaller settlements in the area. They were all covered under thirteen to twenty feet of volcanic ash and pumice. The eruption lasted a mere 18 hours.

Once a major port trading up and down the Italian peninsula, the Greek islands, and North Africa, Pompeii supplied silk, spices, fruits, pottery, and sandalwood. But the eruption changed all that, including the coastline; and the village inland was no more. Its location would remain a mystery for a millennium and a half; inhabitants and their collective property ceased to exist. Herculaneum and other villages suffered the same fate.

First discovered in the 16th century by laborers working for the Italian architect, Domenico Fontana, while digging a canal, it wasn't until 1748 that work began. In 1763 the inscription *Rei publicae Pompeianorum* was unearthed, confirming that it was

Pompeii. Actually, the start became known as the birth of modern archeology.

For the next one hundred years there was looting by treasure seekers and, eventually, the area was divided into sections, debris was cleared and documentation began the orderly process of accounting for the site.

By the 20th century, excavation continued at a steady pace using available technology, but it wasn't till after WWII that intensive excavation took place. By now two-thirds have been excavated, but future uncovering will be slowed down to leave discoveries for future generations.

Because of the almost two millennia that elapsed since that deadly eruption of Vesuvius in 79AD, the finds and discoveries still could surprise you and shock you about the splendor those ancient Pompeians lived.

The well-preserved citadel was protected by the lack of air and moisture for those two thousand years, which allowed for little to no deterioration. Following excavation, the natural and anthropic decline is a constant concern.

On my first visit, we spent a week visiting Pompeii, Herculaneum and the museums in Naples. The visit to Pompeii was overwhelming.

Years later when we went back to Pompeii, new excavations had yielded many more enclosures and the rebuilding was vast. It was truly emotional to visit living rooms, bedrooms; to walk through the rooms and to be aware that 2,000 years before the young and old had lived and enjoyed the village.

Family and friends dining, playing and decorating the now clean murals

I have never forgotten my visits there. Its mystery and magical atmosphere, which I once felt as I walked through paved, dirt roads, today draw me, once more. The melancholy is there as I look at the photos I then took.

As I always do, I kept photographs and notes in my travel journal. I also wrote several poems dedicated to that mysterious hamlet, its people, its many gods and ghosts. So, at last, afraid I could misplace them, I decided to share them with the world.

Ruins of Pompeii with Vesuvius as background

Public buildings

Temple of Apollo with Vesuvius in background

Aphrodite from the House of Mars

Aphrodite

Apollo

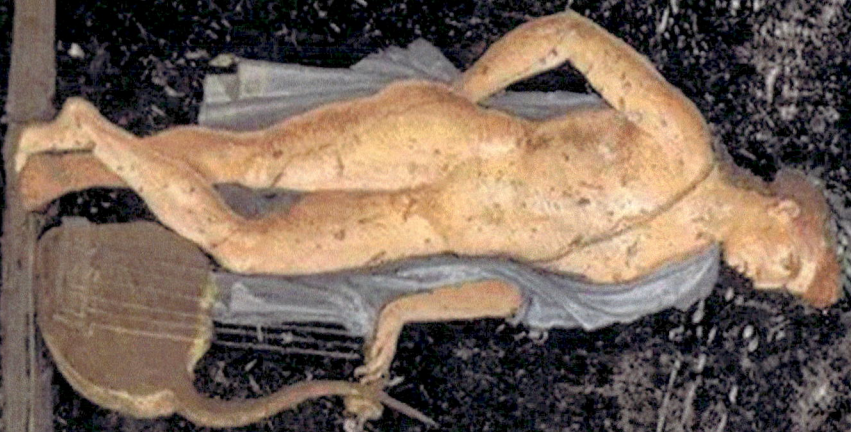

Apollo and Cassandra

Basilica (public building)

Cupids (House of Vettii)

The Forum

Via of the Abundance

Lupanar (brothel)

Satyr from House of the Vettii

Satyr and maenad (House of Caecilius)

FATE

Decades gathering wealth
laboring many hours
developing a lineage
and a taste for the arts
for the finer things

Sacrifices
to leave your children
in a better world
Now we understand
parental yearnings
through millennia
do not change

Immortal divinities
tumbling down
on a serene afternoon
when nature decided what course
your life would take, instead

Soon realizing
there was no protection
from man-made gods
Wasted offerings
Painful to accept
death makes us equal

LETHAL

The meek shall inherit the earth
Or will they?
The fumes were not selective
penetrating the bronchi
of merchants, nobles, sinners, the pious...
Women, children, men, animals...
tamed and beast...
fell under ash, pumice...
and blisteringly hot gasses...
Wholesale, aimless death

FORTUNA

Goddess of fortune, dispenser of luck
where were you on that fatal day
when the village was burning?
Screeching owls
left without a nest
were the only witnesses
to survive and tell
Cornucopia found empty at
Via dell'Abbondanza

Villagers who believed in
miracles took a chance
remained against all odds
giving up the harvest
was not a choice

Empty guidance without warning
darkness covered
the eyes of your devotees
sealed tight for eternity

VESUVIUS

With cyclopean precision and
scorching thunderbolts, the
monster covered its crime
fire, lava, ash, pumice...
Fumes veiled
a classical village back in 79 A.D.
Pompeii stopped playing the flute
drinking wine, praying
and bearing offering
to the gods for preservation
Then flesh vanished under mud and basalt
Yesterday wind and soft rain
trailed me the second time
I explored the grounds
and traced images of me
with Vesuvius at my back
Spotted Helios' chariot, bleak, riderless
East to west was veiled in shadows
as I strolled quivering and drenched
taking cover in House of Meander
The village, calm, bluish-gray
for a moment I thought of rumblings
the ancient fumarole breathing
warning the intruder
Ocherous, latent
still alive and waiting
to strike with the force of a thousand bombs
infuriated by dusty intruders
digging up life of those who had laid
silently beneath the earth

PROMISES

Beware of Greeks bearing gifts
Mortals accepting deities' pledge of
baskets full of bread and wine — intoxicating

Where were you, celestial being
the afternoon of the cataclysm?
Volcanic lava rained down
in tranquil Pompeii
Did you see it?

Your exit left us unprotected
Ready to feast in another village?
Same promises. Same aftereffect perhaps?
Staying through bonanza
till darken days again
divines vanish without a trace

VIA DEI SEPOLCRI

Besides our fashionable villas, there
in the sepulchers we lay
one mausoleum larger than the next
We need to show
our neighbors we were — once
perfection incarnate

To overlook our virtuous lives
and each step we had purposely taken
Those who knew us
and friends we favor now
must sanction our glorious deeds
otherwise
What would be the purpose
of having lived?

DESTINY

Clotho and Lachesis had entered their abode
delicately unwinding their golden threads
and were received with cheers
But on that night, grief was upon them
all was nebulous, as the Parcae
garbed in cascading robes, paid a visit
Curiously, this time only Atropos appeared
with purpose. She moved swiftly,
one dwelling after another
The cries of children didn't stirred her
This deity was on a terminal mission
And nothing could detained this daughter
of darkness
Not the vow a new shrine
Helplessness and perplexity
invaded the zealots
She breezed by enticingly, shears in hand
ready to sever
prematurely
binding threads
to the terra firma of their ancestors
All was gone
Determination accomplished
They were the last to exit

CREDO

On the eve before sadness set in
common villagers and the gods collided in a union
of the sacred and the profane

Then a surrealistic spectacle was enacted at
Villa of the Mysteries
Here Dionysus
offer to the maidens was wine
and the lighthearted Sileni sang, played
the lyre, as a young man
sounded the pipes lent by Pan

Overcome with ecstasy, a woman danced
while another brought a phallus into the room
They all took turns in orgasmic feast
symbol of fecundity
as others shared winsome poetry

Rubbing blood of an hapless goat
blood seeped sluggishly into
crevices and clefts
and they became one and the same

Eternally filled by the twice-born
Devotees without boundaries
in the name of good wine
and an excellent harvest, danced
frenetically
Flagellated women kept on dancing
possessed by the god of pleasure

Happiness and laughter was the end
in an intoxicated first century
Numbness first suggested by the Supreme
and everything was joy till earth
put an end to festivities
Gobblers cracked into tiny pieces
spirits covered the ground
Wailing, perplexing, disillusion
to the few who survived
purification ceremonies
could not change the course of death

EXCESS

Fortuna, where were you that lethal night
when the village was aflame?
The villagers believed in you
took a chance
against all odds
refused to release the soil
the harvest they had gathered
with your guidance
Cries, screeching, howls
birds without nests
corpses
Then you steered your vessel
To favored lands
when the eyes of your devotees
sealed for eternity

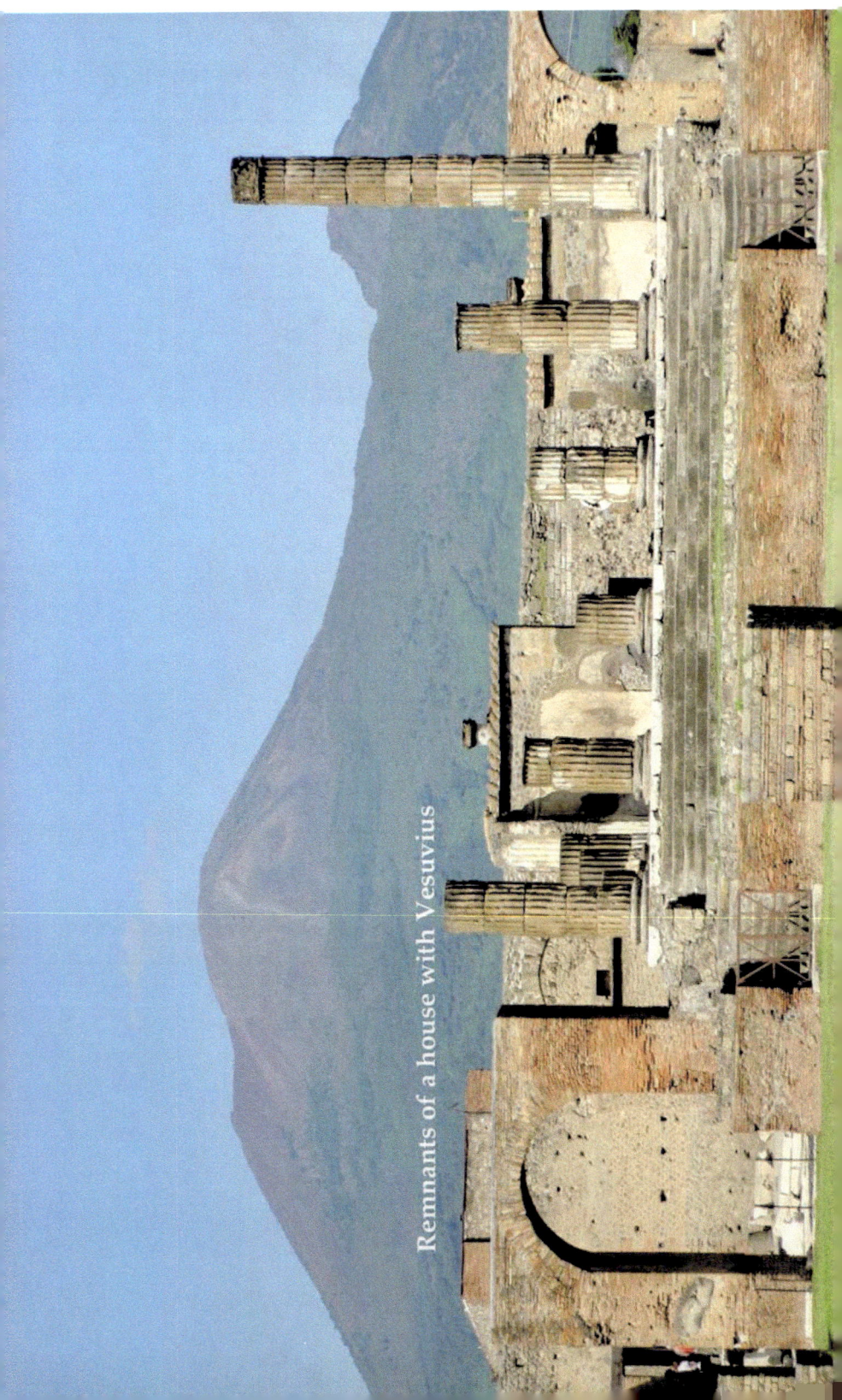

Remnants of a house with Vesuvius

City street

Bakery

Apollo

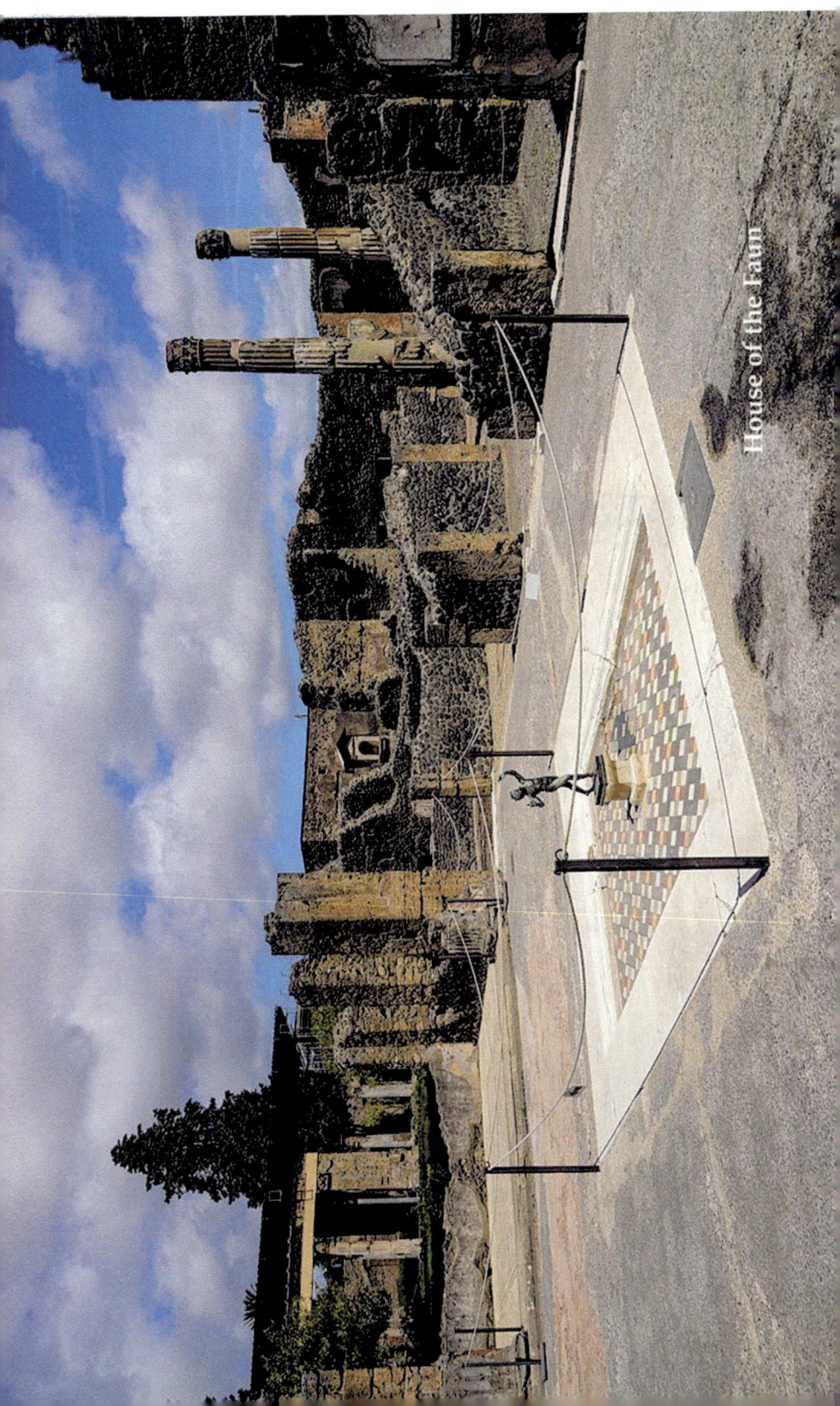
House of the Faun

City street

City street

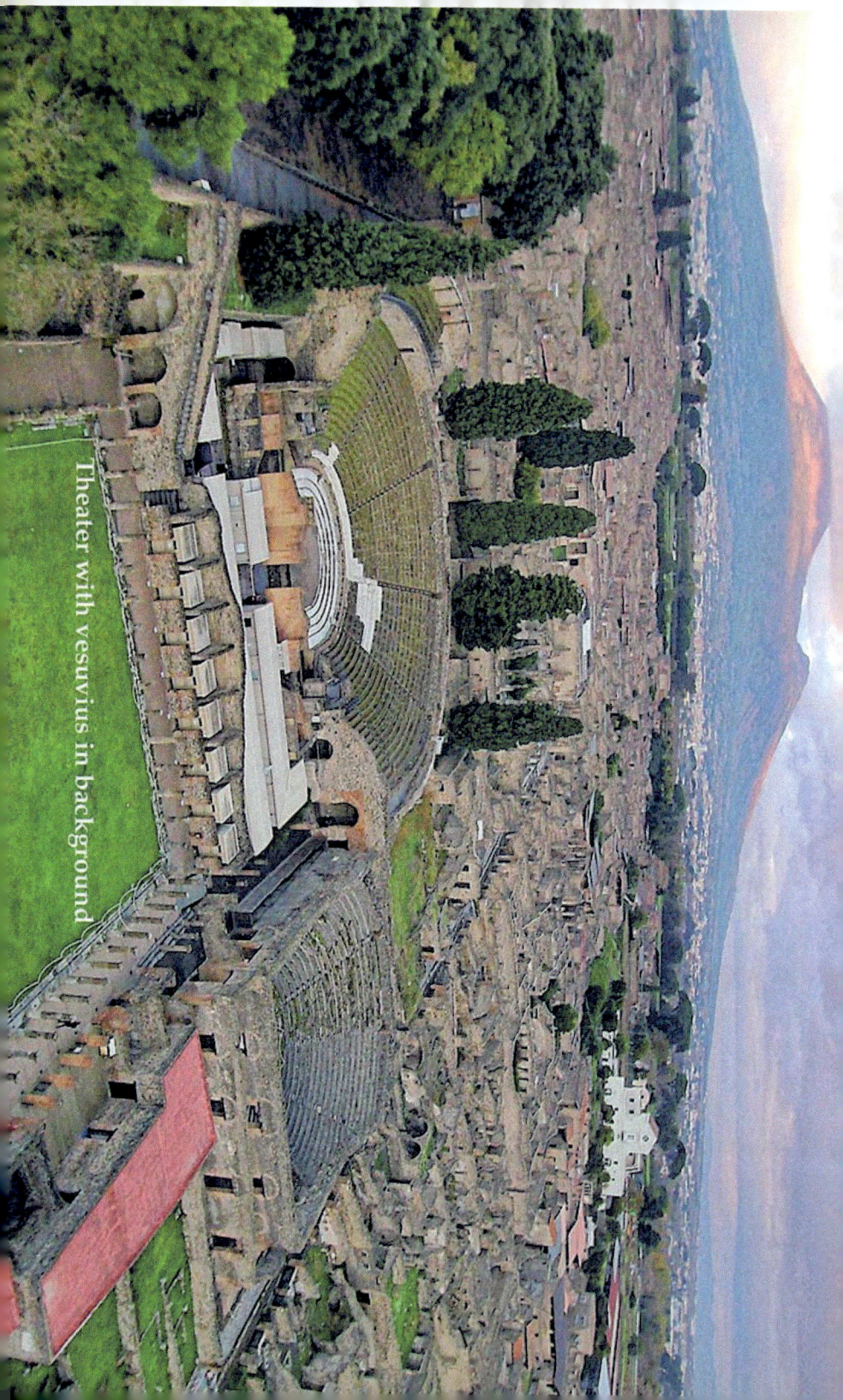
Theater with vesuvius in background

Helen of Troy and Paris

House of Meleager

The Villa of the Mysteries

The Villa of the Mysteries

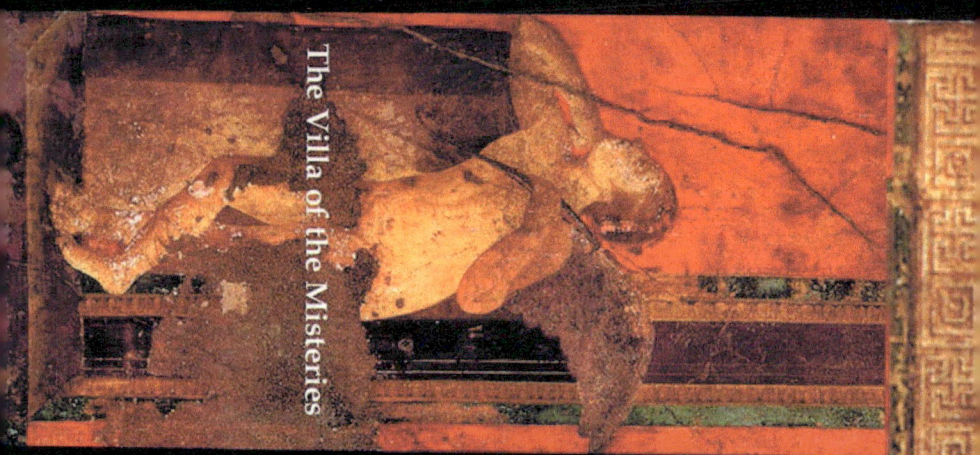

The Villa of the Misteries

CLOUDS

Oh, Pompeii!
dark days upon us
Pledges to the gods
glorious deeds
with nothing to show
The honor and virtue of the dead
could not silence
Vesuvius

SENSE

What it was:
Night before the eruption
A euphoric Bacchus
dancing with Bacchantes
Semele and Jupiter
beholding the revelry
with pride and amusement
But Ariadne, wise beyond words
autumn chestnut leaves
weaving through her hair
sat unspooling the thread
that would guide them
out of the scorching village

LINUS' FLUTE CONCERT

We met under the portico at Stabian Baths
we broke the rules and
you recited sweet rhymes
No need for a *praefurnium*
to keep us warm
Priapus took the lead
Aphrodite danced in foam
a bewildered Apollo looked on
Swift as a gladiator
ready to entertain
you traveled north to south
discovering my flesh
aromatic petals camouflaging nudity
Seemingly, Vesuvius approving our
stance
Indiscipline was no concern
disharmony our objective
Our tryst was secure
no mysteries or angst
Timeless bodies unrestrained
through centuries
Pleasure our aim
one and only

BENEATH OUR FEET

Pliny the Younger
met me at the gate
to relate the story
of turbulent days

GUARDIANS

Jupiter, Juno, and Minerva
unable to stop
The great eruption
destroyed their homes

Volcanic debris covering fields
two thousand good people
and their pets
perished under cinders
emerging from earth

RESURRECTION

On the tragic third day
the sun had broken through
to tug at heartstrings
once more
Buried in ash
Nothing to do for the few who survived
walking away worn out, mournful
empty handed
Via Porta Ercolano the getaway
giving the gods a rest

ASHES

Casts of victims all around me
Seemly empty
yet filled with souls

They paid tribute
to the sun, earth, the sea each day
visited temples
as instructed for millennia

Then I dared to lightly touch
the cast of a man
stretched out over a woman
A cloak cladding their faces
a last effort to shield her
from the fumes
Powerful tremors journeyed up my spine
his spirit was professing
the flesh had dissolved but
love
more potent
than fear
would roam devotedly for eternity.

BLUE HYACINTH FOR THE TRAGIC POET

On my last visit
early in a peaceful morning
I woke up
rushed to your door
to place clusters of blue hyacinths
I had gather in the wild fields
of the Sarno Valley
unscathed by Vesuvius
Rejecting departure
till offering a memento
in the urn at your gate
I left the flowers
An oblation to the gods
to allow me a return
to satisfy my verse with your grace
as I once had indulged in years past

GREEK AND ROMAN GODS CITED

Aphrodite: Greek goddess of love

Apollo: Greek god of archery, music and dance, truth and prophecy, healing and diseases, light, poetry...

Atropos: Greek goddess of fate and destiny (death)

Ariadne: Greek goddess of labyrinths

Bacchus: Roman god of agriculture, wine and fertility. (Greek Dionysus).

Clotho: Greek goddess of fate and destiny (the spinner of human life).

Dionysus: Greek god of agriculture, wine and fertility.

Fortuna: Roman goddess of luck

Helios: Greek god of the sun

Juno: Roman goddess of marriage and childbirth

Jupiter: Roman king of the gods. Chief deity

Lachesis: Greek goddess of fate and destiny (the allotter of human life).

Minerva: Roman virgin goddess of music, poetry, medicine, wisdom, commerce, weaving, and the crafts...

Pan: Greek god of the wild, shepherds, and fertility

Parcae: Roman female personifications of destiny

Priapus: Greek god of animal and vegetable fertility

Semele: Greek goddess of the earth, mother of Dionysus.

Sileni: Greek class of wild nature spirits and companions of the wine god Dionysus.